A Concise Guide To

Better Decisions

The key tools for better decision making and failure proofing your life.

Tony Pray, PMP

A Publication of

FAPray.com

TotalRecall Publications, Inc.
1103 Middlecreek
Friendswood, Texas 77546
281-992-3131 281-482-5390 Fax
www.totalrecallpress.com

All rights reserved. Except as permitted under the United States Copyright Act of 1976, no part of this publication may be reproduced, stored in a retrieval system, or transmitted in any form or by any means electronic or mechanical or by photocopying, recording, or otherwise without prior permission of the publisher. Exclusive worldwide content publication / distribution by TotalRecall Publications, Inc.

© Copyright 2020, by Tony Pray.
Book Cover Design: Bruce Moran

ISBN: 978-1-59095-5222
UPC: 6-43977-55226-6

Printed in the United States of America with simultaneous printings in Australia, Canada, and United Kingdom.

FIRST EDITION

1 2 3 4 5 6 7 8 9 10

This is a non fiction work.
The scanning, uploading, and distribution of this book via the Internet or via any other means without the permission of the publisher is illegal and punishable by law. Please purchase only authorized electronic editions, and do not participate in or encourage electronic piracy of copyrighted materials. Your support of the author's rights is appreciated.

Table of Contents

Introduction

Chapter 1: Why Decisions Go Wrong
Chapter 2: Before The Decision
Chapter 3: Define The Problem
Chapter 4: Expand The Options
Chapter 5: Filter The Options
Chapter 6: Learn From Results
Chapter 7: Conclusion
Chapter 8: Resources

Introduction

Your Concise Guide To Better Decisions

Would you appreciate learning a better approach to decision making? One that can be applied broadly to almost any decision and <u>will improve the outcome</u>? I've distilled years of experience and research into good decision making.

You won't find an in-depth technical exploration of the bits and pieces that go into good decisions. There are plenty of resources that will explain things like Monte Carlo simulations, Bayesian reasoning and statistical analysis. You will find key tools you can use immediately.

- **Distill content to the essential:** Following the 80/20 rule, I don't throw every possible tool in the kit but I do cover the essentials.
- **Explain how each part fits**
- **Arrange it so it makes a coherent whole**
- **Put it into digestible chunks**
- **Give you a better toolkit for any decision**

Making better decisions is a process which you can think of like a computer algorithm. Stepping through a good process, selecting the steps that apply to your decision, implementing the decision and looping back after the decision to improve the algorithm creates a positive feedback loop. As you gain experience using the process, your decisions will improve.

This book is a step-by step guide through the process.

1

CHAPTER ONE

Why Decisions Go Wrong

In This Chapter

1. We are all human
2. Biases affect everyone
3. Imagining unknowns
4. Probabilistic thinking
5. Doing the math

> *To make mistakes or be wrong is human. To admit those mistakes shows you have the ability to learn, and are growing wiser.*
>
> — Donald L. Hicks, Look into the stillness

We Are All Human

> "There is nothing wrong with ***making*** mistakes, but one should always make ***new*** ones. ***Repeating*** mistakes is a hallmark of dim consciousness."
>
> \- **Dave Sim**

All human beings make most decisions subconsciously. We very seldom direct effort into making conscious decisions because it costs us mental energy and it is much slower. We evolved to make quick decisions in circumstances which could be life threatening and the person who shied away at quick movement might have looked and felt silly, but that person survived when the predator actually attacked. Today that same person is subject to hundreds if not thousands of stimuli each day that trigger a response that kicks stress hormones into the system, but none of them is deadly.

Human beings are well adapted to the environment we lived in for millions of years… not so much so for today's world. We are built to **come up very quickly with answers and then to come up with the reasons** to justify them. This is fine for most decisions and saves a lot of mental energy. What it doesn't do is to handle complex, decisions in the modern era which need the much slower, more effortful, deliberate and conscious type of decision.

Should you jump back from the alligator? Oops, too late. You stopped to think about it.

Should you merge your company with your competitor? Oops, too quick. You didn't stop to think about it. More to the point, you need to think about it in a disciplined way that maximizes your chance for success.

Modern neuroscience is now confirming many of the theories that evolutionary biologists produced in the last few decades. We are hard wired with a large number (over 100 have been identified so far) of biases. These biases weight our decisions in ways that aren't logical but which made sense in evolutionary terms.

Biases affect everyone

Confirmation bias affects us all. Scientists are extremely aware of confirmation bias. That is why a large part of the scientific method includes **seeking out disconfirming evidence.** Scientific publications are subject to **rigorous peer review** when other scientists are expected to look at the evidence and tear apart the arguments for a given theory.

The gold standard for a scientific result is that it has been tested and reproduced by unrelated researchers in **replicated controlled double-blind** studies. All of this effort is required to remove as much confirmation bias as possible. This is true even for scientists who are painfully aware for our confirmation bias.

There are hundreds of other biases affecting our judgement that we need to tame in order to **get to the optimal decision** in today's version of the savannah. Have a look at [Wikipedia's](#) entry for bias. They affect all of us to some degree and even when we are aware of the bias in others, we can't see it or compensate for it in ourselves.

Among the many biases we share, **the availability bias** forces us to consider things which are extremely unlikely but which are sensational or attention grabbing to be much more likely than they are. People stayed out of the ocean in droves after the movie "*Jaws*" came out. The chances of being bitten by a shark are far lower than the chance of a traffic accident on the way to the beach.

People think murder is more common than suicide even though suicides are twice as common as murders. This bias is made worse with the media's "If it bleeds it leads" focus. We generally believe things are worse than they actually are because these things are immediately available for our recall.

Absurdity bias: Events that have never happened are not recalled, and hence deemed to have probability zero. When no flooding has recently occurred (and yet the probabilities are still fairly calculable), people refuse to buy flood insurance even when it is heavily subsidized and priced far below an actuarially fair value.

Planning Fallacy: People systematically underestimate the time it will take to accomplish any complex task because we tend to always estimate based on the best case scenario. There is a fairly reliable way to fix the planning fallacy, if you're doing something broadly similar to a reference class of previous projects. Just ask how long similar projects have taken in the past, without considering any of the special properties of this project. Better yet, ask an experienced outsider how long similar projects have taken.

> "It is useless to attempt to reason a man out of a thing he was never reasoned into.".
>
> — Jonathan Swift

Biases affect everyone

Hindsight bias: This occurs when people who know the answer vastly overestimate its predictability or obviousness, compared to the estimates of subjects who must guess without advance knowledge. Hindsight bias is sometimes called the I-knew-it-all-along effect. Very difficult to avoid unless the predictions you make are properly recorded in advance so the decision process can be judged based on what was known at the time of the prediction or decision.

Expecting Short Inferential Distances: Many times it takes more than one step to get from a listener's current understanding to a new level of understanding. However, we have been conditioned by both evolution and our ancestral environment to expect explanations to be just a step or two. A clear argument has to lay out an inferential pathway, starting from what the audience already knows or accepts. If you don't take the recursion far enough, you're just talking to yourself. Explain in advance that it's a multiple step argument or you leave your audience behind.

Loss Aversion Bias: the perception that a loss does greater harm than the gain from an equal good. For example, given the chance on a coin flip to either win $100 or lose $50, most people will decline the bet. This bias prevents us from taking calculated risks that are very good bets. Often seen in combination with the sunk cost fallacy (say that your first time, you accepted the bet and lost $50, most people would be extremely reluctant to take the chance a second time). Do the math and, assuming the numbers are right, take the calculated risks that can pay off appropriately.

Sunk Cost Fallacy: The belief that, because something has taken serious amounts of time, money or effort that it should be continued and even more invested in it when it is a failure. Recognize sunk costs and proceed with no regard to them.

There are hundreds of biases which may need to be accounted for in an optimal decision process. Some will always apply and some will only affect certain well defined situations. Biases are neither good nor bad in most everyday decisions. They help us by reducing the amount of effort needed for many decisions but if not taken into account, they will trip us.

"Of course, this could also be confirmation bias from me wanting you to get sick."

Imagining unknowns

> When "Things go wrong", have a plan to deal with them in the most effective manner possible, as early as possible.
>
> \- **Tony Pray**

We all have difficulty with imagining the extremely unusual "perfect storm" set of events that can cause catastrophes. If any of the dozens of things in the chain of events had been different, the Chernobyl disaster would never have happened. Our imaginations fail us.

The nuclear disaster at the Fukushima, Japan site was caused on the other hand by problems that had been foreseen in the design. No human error there except that of underestimating the size of the tidal wave that could be produced by such a large earthquake. Again, our imaginations failed us.

We remember those events because of the catastrophes they created. The rare but extremely impactful events are called "black swans" or for those of you into statistics, "long tail" events.

We are simply not built to handle them. We suffer from too short a time horizon in our imaginations, too many permutations of possibilities to predict all of them and other priorities which demand our attention.

So for any consequential decision, all we can do is to reduce the risks, never completely eliminate them. We can simplify things as much as possible since complexity always increases risk. We can create reserves of money, time and resources to cover as many of the "unknowns" as possible. For the "unknown unknowns" we can make the decision as resilient as possible.

Sometimes even the best decisions, made with incomplete information, will turn out badly. **You only need to revisit your decision process if it turns out that the decision was bad** and there's something in the process which can be improved to address that flaw.

Probability Thinking

 **There are lies, damned lies and statistics.**

- **Mark Twain**

The headline reads "Cancer risk raised 50% with the use of shampoo!" The Internet immediately pounces and the common ingredient Sodium Laureth Sulfate, used in many shampoos, is identified as the culprit. Soon warnings are appearing everywhere to avoid the use of any shampoo containing this chemical. The evening news reports that the makers of the chemical are being sued by hundreds of cancer patients.

Sound plausible or even familiar? It should. This scare has been circulating on the Internet since the 1980s. A quick check at Snopes.com will tell you that this detergent, used as a foaming agent in toothpaste, shampoo and even in garage floor cleaners is not a cancer causing chemical. It can be a minor irritant and you will want to rinse your eyes if you get any there but the only harmful effect from it if you actually drink it is diarrhea!

There are a number of biases that make it more likely we'll agree. It is a scary statement and it's easy to remember. The availability bias will bring it to mind. Most people don't check the credibility of the sources and assume that they are doing the right thing by warning their friends. The friends in turn received the information from someone they trust who is part of their own "in" group. It soon becomes the sort of thing that "our" sort of people knows to be true. This is much like the often discredited theory that vaccines cause autism.

Bogus math ahead...

Another problem we have is that our ability think in probabilities is very poor. When you read the headline about the 50% rise in the risk of cancer, did it cause you to pause for a moment. That's a HUGE jump... or is it? Think of it this way. If the normal rate of a particular type of cancer is 2 people in 100,000 and the rate of the same cancer in the shampoo using group is 3 people in 100,000, isn't that a 50% increase in risk? Yet overall the amount of risk is tiny.

Think about the margin for error of even the best controlled, double-blind studies. Let's assume that the margin for error in this case was only 1%. We'd need to have more than 10 cases of cancer in this group to even exceed the margin of error. That would mean an increase of 500%.

Probability Thinking

We are all subject to thinking errors and probabilities are one area where we truly don't have good intuition. In the example above. An increase from 2 to 3 is certainly a 50% increase. However the overall risk was actually the increase from 2/100,000 to 3/100,000 or from .00002 to .00003. That works out to a 1 tenth of one percent increase in risk. With a 1 percent error margin (not to mention the confidence level that would be assigned to any legitimate study) this is considered the "noise" in the signal.

If you get the raw numbers, your intuition has a much better chance of getting hold of the truth. If you don't know what the baseline numbers are, you can't really tell what's being compared.

When you can do so, look at the raw numbers. Our intuitive grasp of them is much better and it's harder to manipulate perceptions.

2

CHAPTER TWO

Before The Decision

In This Chapter

1. Eliminate Stupid
2. Know your strategy
3. Limit your losses

Eliminate Stupid

> "It is remarkable how much long-term advantage people like us have gotten by trying to be consistently not stupid, instead of trying to be very intelligent."
> **Charlie Munger**

Avoid making stupid mistakes. **If you can accomplish this single task for all of your business decisions, you will have greatly improved your odds of success.** If you spend the time to eliminate only the glaring mistakes, your chances of success increase dramatically. It is better to spend energy on eliminating these types of mistakes than to spend the same energy looking for an "optimal" solution.

These are things which will predictably make us forget or overlook important things. **Be even more cautious if you are affected by more than one of these.** These are conditions which reliably add to stupidity.

1. Being outside of your circle of competence or area of true expertise or trusting the input of others who are outside their circle of compctence.
2. Stress, exhaustion, rushing or urgency
3. Fixation on a particular outcome
4. Information overload, especially including overload of short term memory
5. Multitasking (There is no such thing, we just switch between tasks quickly and always at a cost in terms of our mental capacity) Do one thing at a time.
6. Being in a group where social cohesion comes into play. This is especially true whenever one is asked to declare loyalty to a group by accepting a particular "article of faith" with no proof. Groupthink is an example.
7. Being in the presence of an "authority." Many authorities in one area express opinions in other areas where they truly have no right to an opinion.
8. Failure to have competent others review the decision.

Eliminate Stupid

Define the perimeter of your circle of competence, and operate inside it. Over time, work to expand that circle but never fool yourself about where it stands today, and never be afraid to say "I don't know."

Vet your advisors thoroughly to make sure they have earned the right to have an opinion in this particular domain. Know what level of confidence you assign to their input.

If you are under intense stress, tired or working with extreme urgency, make sure to be aware that this is taking points off of your IQ. Understand how stress can cause us to overlook the obvious and forget the important in favor of the most urgent.

Take the time to rest and do justice to this decision. Try to take on the most important / difficult tasks early in the day, before you are tired.

Sometimes we all seem to "know" that the best outcome is not what the facts that are easily presented will support. Be wary of your own hidden agendas. Either find a way to express those hidden facts or stay with what the facts are telling you.

Too much information, presented too quickly will cause you to be unable to distinguish the trivial from the essential. Your mind needs time to digest "chunks" of new information and to integrate it with the rest of your understanding.

Don't fool yourself into thinking you truly understand something just because it made sense when it was explained to you. Can you put aside any books and notes and effectively describe the problem to be solved, the "why" the problem needs to be solved and the arguments for each proposed solution to a lay person? If you can do that you probably have a good grip on the issue.

Avoiding the situations that make us stupid raises the level of your decision making.

Preventing the simple stupid mistakes should also have a larger payoff with less effort than "optimizing" your decisions.

Know Your Strategy

Learning from my mistakes since 1952 just so I could share with you.

Tony Pray

I'm in the midst of moving my blog onto my own host. I have a million things I need to <u>eventually</u> do to get this blog perfected. I also need to write real content for the blog and maintain things on the home front. While Donna's knee replacement heals I'm picking up the housework Donna normally does and that's a lot.

I've let myself get a bit overwhelmed. So I needed to stop and take a few minutes to do a reset and focus on getting my current list of priorities straight. So, here's the process I walked myself through:

1. **Eliminate stupid** -See the previous pages
2. Remember my **strategy and overall goals**. My intent is to share the knowledge and wisdom I've distilled out of my experiences over the past 67 years with you and to make it fun to read.
3. **Prioritize** the decisions I need to make based on how much they can move the needle on the things that matter.
4. **Reduce any down side** as possible, including time spent on low priorities
5. **Tackle the top priority**.
6. Note the results and when needed, **improve the process**.
7. Once I finish moving priority 1 as far as I can today... **lather, rinse, repeat**.

Before you make any decisions, **determine your overall goals and priorities**. See if the things you're spending time on will contribute to those goals. It's fine to wander aimlessly if you have no particular thing you want to do. If you have a goal in mind, it's best to wander in the right general direction.

Following the steps above **creates a positive feedback loop** where each round of decisions raises the bar slightly to improve the next one.

Limit Loss

> "Many people take no care of their money till they come nearly to the end of it, and others do just the same with their time."
>
> —Johann Wolfgang von Goethe

You can do things to limit your downside risk for almost any decision you make. If you make it a practice to **always limit the downside and enhance the upside** in your decisions, over time you can't help but do better.

To limit loss, there are strategies such as insurance, dipping a toe in the water (doing a small pilot of an idea for example), avoiding any risk whose payoff isn't worth the risk or preparing to absorb damage in a way that won't cripple you. Some kinds of downside can't be avoided but must be absorbed and accepted.

Before you engage in a big decision, start a huge project or make irrevocable changes, **limit your losses.** When I go to a casino, I know in advance how much I am willing to lose for the evening's entertainment. I set a limit to my losses.

When I start on a personal project, I know how much time I'm willing to invest before I commit to the project. **Loss of time is a waste of your most valuable asset.**

You can engage classic risk management strategies such as hedging, insurance, risk reduction, sharing the risk with others, avoiding the risks altogether (impossible to do for unknown risks) and having contingency plans and funds.

Know how much money, time or other resources you are willing to chance on this decision. Define that up front, even before you know much detail about the decision to be made. **Set the limit and set triggers which warn you when the limit is approaching**.

Truly, this section should be in the "Eliminate Stupid" pages but I think it is important enough that it warrants a page of its' own.

3

CHAPTER THREE

Define The Problem

In This Chapter

1. What is the problem to be solved?
2. Why is the decision needed?
3. Decision Log
4. Clear problem statement
5. Stakeholders engaged
6. Success and failure criteria defined

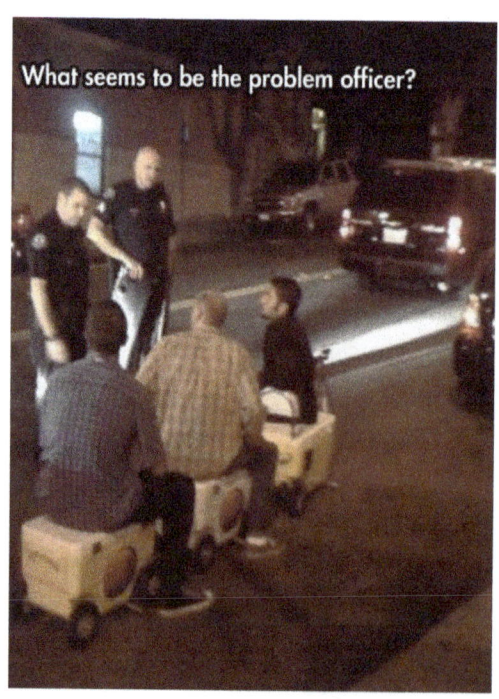

What is the problem to be solved?

 *"Asking a question is the simplest way of focusing thinking...asking the right question may be the most important part of thinking."*

Edward de Bono

Frame the Decision

As you create your initial hypotheses, make sure that narrow framing of the decision isn't an issue. Ask the right question.

There is **very seldom a strictly binary decision** needed. Often the framing of the problem to be solved/decision to be made will heavily influence what possibilities are even considered.

Take a step back from the way the problem is initially presented and you can **avoid the "Availability bias"**. This bias pops up in many situations where you have partial information and those thoughts that are most often immediately available get emphasis while harder to recall items don't get considered.

Determine if there are approaches other than those initially presented which might work. **Can aspects of one option be combined with another** to provide a more optimized solution? Reframe the decision from an adversary's viewpoint.

Try this exercise – assume that you have several options but in the end you will not be able to choose any of them. What would you do next? **Widen the framework.**

Considering what fleet vehicle to buy – reframe the question as "How to reliably get my employees where they need to be? It might be that taking Uber is your best alternative but wouldn't have been considered if you kept the question framed too narrowly.

Make sure that you are answering the right question.

Once you have framed the decision broadly, **include the "Do Nothing" option** if it is possible among the available choices. There is always an opportunity cost with any actions you take. Would your resources be better used elsewhere?

Create a testable hypothesis

Finally, after setting the general frame for the decision, you need to **make each option in the decision tree into a testable hypothesis.** This will allow you to test and validate your approaches to the decision.

Test or pilot your decision options to determine the optimum solution. This also will help to eliminate the confirmation bias and will give you real world data to defend the outcome.

Why is the decision needed?

The 5 "Whys"

Ask yourself why this decision is needed. What is the business reason for it. How does it support your overall strategy. Ask yourself "why" and when you get the first answer, ask why again until you **understand the root of the problem** that you are trying to address.

Decision Scope – How much time and energy needs to be spent on the decision?

Is the decision bigger than a breadbox? Is it a career making (or ending) decision, or a run of the mill analysis?

It makes no sense to over analyze small, inconsequential decisions. If the impact of this decision is minimal, then use the 1 Page Decision process to make a reasonably good decision. Save full due diligence for something much more impactful.

Decision Log

Create a Decision Log file or other tracking note system so you can track through, review and communicate the decision and the process you used to reach it. Use it to record your progress. Memories fade and it can be impossible to track too many threads of information. Capture the decision to be made, the options you start with, reasons options are rejected as you filter them, weighting scores as you measure risks, benefits, pros and cons for each option and results of the decision. Use the information in the log to improve the process.

Know what question you are actually asking.

Create a clear problem statement.
Describe the decision needed or statement of the problem to solve: NOTE: Is it something a 10 year old can understand? If you can't explain it to a child, you probably don't understand the need well enough. Make sure you express the problem to be solved in terms of why it needs to be solved.

Define your success criteria: What are the minimum conditions which will indicate that the decision has been successful or the problem is fully or partially solved?

What are your failure criteria:
What conditions will indicate the decision should be abandoned or revisited?

Is this a time sensitive decision? If so, set the deadline

Who is impacted? **Involve these stakeholders** in the decision process. Getting them involved early in the process will not guarantee they'll be happy with the final outcome but it will guarantee they'll be heard and their issues considered in the final decision. This often makes their buy-in possible.

List any known alternative approaches or solutions.

Add alternatives as needed.

List the key criteria that need to be considered for successful decision (e.g. for deciding on a car purchase- mileage, passenger capacity, style, cost, comfort, safety)

Prioritize and weight the criteria with any minimums or maximums noted
(e.g. in a car purchase, maximum cost $45k, minimum mileage 20mpg, 5 star safety rating.)

Put the information into your decision log. This is your starting point and will help you communicate to others when the time comes.

4

CHAPTER FOUR

Expand The Options

In This Chapter

1. Consider the "Do Nothing" option
2. Invert the problem
3. Brainstorm effectively
4. Look for partial solutions and recombine options
5. Get expert advice
6. Benchmark
7. Wear different hats
8. Baloney Detection

 *"So many roads. So many detours. So many choices. So many mistakes."*

Sarah Jessica Parker

The "Do Nothing" Option

Very few decisions are strictly binary in nature. In many cases, the "Do This Or Do That" option can also be expanded to **include "Do Nothing"** and "Do a Combination of This and That". Doing nothing at all about a particular situation can be difficult to defend, since we all have a bias toward action. If you understand the risks, benefits, opportunity cost and return on investment of your options, including the "Do Nothing" option, you'll be able to defend your choice.

Brainstorming

One way to expand the options is by **brainstorming**. Please be careful here to **make sure that this is a "safe" environment** to voice even silly options. The ability to open and discuss off-the-wall solutions can be severely limited by people's natural tendency to not appear frivolous in front of the boss. Sometimes it's a good idea to remove the authority figures from the room and let people free wheel with ideas. **Sometimes the silly ideas trigger really useful ideas**.

Another way to expand options is to have the team members each **write down at least 3 approaches** without referring to each others' answers.

Think from different perspectives, e.g. time-to-market, financial, manageability, technical ease of implementation, resource use. **What's the minimum viable option look like?**

Learn from people who have already solved your problem... Benchmark!

Benchmarking, whether from an internal group that shines in a particular area or from an external competitor or other company that faces similar issues is a great way to discover better approaches to your decision.

Experts in this particular domain can be counted upon for accurate baseline and historical information but keep in mind that they are no more accurate in making predictions than a simple algorithm that just plots existing trends forward.

Wear Different Hats

Examine alternatives from multiple perspectives:

1. **Invert the problem** - for example instead of trying to find ways to protect your network, think through the ways it can be hacked and ways that you can make it easier to hack, then reverse that process and start building obstacles to those avenues of attack. Think of ways to slow a project, confusing and conflicting goals, bureaucracy, etc. then go about removing those obstacles.
2. **Think from first principles** - what are the physical limitations the universe imposes? Can the decision or alternative be done another way?
3. **Consider secondary effects.** Does this decision produce unintended consequences upstream or downstream? Are there costs being externalized that will come home to roost?
4. **What are the financials. What are the incentives?** Are you creating perverse incentives that don't align with your strategy?
5. Can elements from the options you have created be **combined to create better options**?

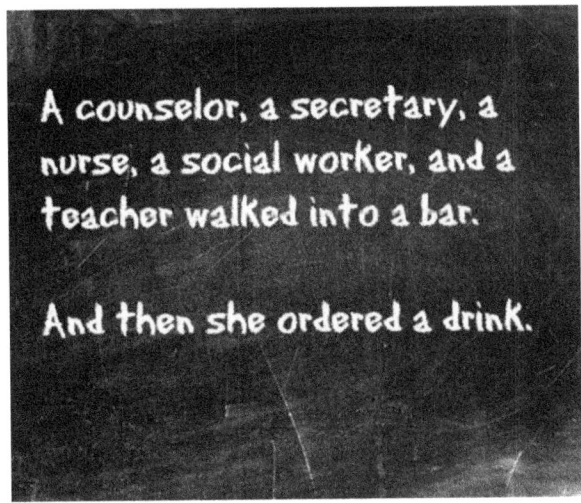

Watch out for Baloney

Baloney Detection - Watch out for errors, omissions, deliberate and accidental lies and exaggeration.

As you evaluate the inputs you'll be getting for your decisions, remember to always be alert for a variety of types of baloney. Of course, there's the garden variety exaggeration, which can be compensated for by weighting the answer appropriately or stating the confidence level as less. There are also the straightforward lies, misrepresentations, obfuscations and errors of fact to be alert for.

People unconsciously lie. For example, asked how long a given task will take and what's the worst case estimate, most people heavily underestimate the time. Even when they consciously add a fudge factor to the estimate, they'll frequently be far off the mark because people generally do not factor in the unknowns that affect them.

Remember that when a thing looks too good to be true, it can sometimes be true but that's not the way to bet.

Robert Heinlein made a valid point when he created the truism "TANSTAAFL" - (**"There ain't no such thing as a free lunch."**) If you follow the money, it will tell you something about the motivations of the people involved. There's nothing wrong with making an honest profit but profit puts incentives in front of people that may not be in your interests.

It's also a good idea to **understand the incentives that a contributor may have that aren't monetary**. Watch out for group think, flattery of the boss, lazy statements backed up by nothing or statistics quoting suspiciously precise numbers because 97.4 percent of lies are backed up with statistics - and they are boldly stated as fact.

Keep in mind that the **burden of proof when someone makes a claim is on the person making that claim**. The bigger the claim, the higher the burden of proof.

Many times lies are unintentional, never ascribe to enemy action that which might be explained by incompetence.

Here's a good source for ways to sort fact from fiction:

"The Baloney Detection Toolkit" - Visit the Skeptic Society website at: https://www.skeptic.com/skepticism-101/baloney-detection-kit-sandwich-infographic/ to see their beautifully done take on how to spot phony claims. The Skeptic Society itself is a great resource for understanding a wide variety of issues from quack medicine to homeopathy to supernatural claims. Well worth the time and effort.

5

CHAPTER FIVE

Filter The Options

In This Chapter

1. Impossible options
2. Opportunity costs
3. The Pros and Cons list
4. Emotional considerations
5. Ethical and moral dimensions
6. Evaluate risks and mitigate negative risks
7. Plan for resilience
8. Sustainability
9. Consider opposing views carefully - Assign a "Devil's Advocate"
10. What must be true for a successful outcome
11. Review with competent others / negotiate and bargain for buy-in
12. Record the decision

> "It pays to keep an open mind, but not so open your brains fall out."
>
> *Carl Sagan*

Filter the options

Remove the <u>Impossible</u> Options

There are many instances of people in business put under pressure to adopt options which are simply impossible. One example is the IT manager told to maintain the installation schedule even though the manufacturer has not shipped the product. Eliminate impossible options as soon as they are identified so you can concentrate on finding options that are possible.

> Opportunity cost is a huge filter in life. If you've got two suitors who are really eager to have you and one is way the hell better than the other, you do not have to spend much time with the other. And that's the way we filter out buying opportunities.
>
> *Charlie Munger*

Stop to consider what else you could be doing with the time /money / resources needed for this decision.

Is there something you could pick which would make **better use of your resources?** Any decision will have opportunity costs so be sure to identify them and determine how you will prioritize things. What opportunities do you give up if you take this option for your decision? Factor the opportunity costs early into your decision process.

If you are passing up an opportunity that's got better profit potential than the one you're working on now, it is a waste of your resources. Just as in life we can pursue only so many things, in business you need to choose your pursuits well. Scattering your efforts by trying to do everything generally results in accomplishing nothing. Focus on the most important thing. Do that. Then you can lather, rinse and repeat.

The Pros and Cons List

For the options which pass the ethical and emotional tests, it's time to evaluate them logically and a simple starting point is the pro and con list.

> "When confronted with two courses of action I jot down on a piece of paper all the arguments in favor of each one, then on the opposite side I write the arguments against each one. Then by weighing the arguments pro and con and cancelling them out, one against the other, I take the course indicated by what remains."
>
> - Benjamin Franklin

This was good advice back then and still holds true today. For simpler decisions with few options, a straightforward pro and con list will often do the job. For more complex decisions with multiple factors, a weighted pro and con list can be a better tool. The weighted list might use any or all of the following headings:

- Option description
- Pro or Con
- Impact (expressed as high, medium or low - helps ferret out the options that disproportionately affect overall results if this choice turns out to be wrong. Sometimes avoiding these kinds of choices is a better overall strategy)
- Best estimate on the correctness of this option
- Confidence in the estimate (based on proven expertise and experience, from zero to 1)

Multiply the factors to provide an overall score. If impact turns out to be high for this option and low for others, consider using the less risky approach.

SWOT - Strength, Weakness, Opportunity, Threat

SWOT analysis lets you view the options from different perspectives and surfaces issues which can derail you.

Emotional Considerations

Gain some emotional distance from any consequential decision. That's why we are often advised to "sleep on it". It's appropriate to consider emotions a valid part of our toolkit and bring emotions into the decision process .

A **very large part of our decision making process is emotional,** subconsciously generated thought. There's a good reason to trust gut instincts in many cases because we evolved over millions of years to make fast accurate judgments. However, we're not living in the conditions which we evolved from and need the slower, analytical process to be engaged.

Ideally you need a **two-pronged approach** to any consequential decision. One is the logical, emotion free, facts only approach. The other is the emotional, how does it make people feel, is it right for you/your company approach. Take emotional reactions into serious consideration but don't ignore or override the data driven approach.

When a particular option just "feels right", take the time to imagine **what would have to be true for that decision to be 100% right.** Compare that to the things which would have to be true for the other options. When options are roughly equivalent analytically, go with the option that feels right. When an option feels wrong, pin down the reason and keep it in mind.

Include the affected stakeholders in the decision process, allowing them some input into the process and bargaining with them in good faith all will help to gain broader acceptance of the eventual decision.

What are the emotional effects? How is each major stakeholder affected. Can the emotions be reconciled? Can they be used to help drive change?

Behavioral psychologists recognize that **we make MOST decisions emotionally.** Things such as fear of missing out, aversion to loss and social pressure susceptibility can be used to derail progress or, with some imagination, be used to trigger constructive progress. The entire marketing and advertising industry is based on these emotional manipulations. Be aware of them and use them if needed to drive positive change.

Ethics

> "Ethics are more important than laws."
> - *Wynton Marsalis*

Consider the ethical dimensions. Are there any elements that would have trouble passing the "sniff test"? Is there any chance if this decision was to be published in the largest forum possible by factual but very unsympathetic reporters, could there be **any appearance of a lack of ethics**?

Would everyone you care about approve of this decision? Could this decision hurt your company's reputation? Are you adding to anyone's suffering? Are you diminishing anyone's chances to have a better life?

If none of the above apply, then proceed ...

If any of the questions above is still failing the ethical test, remember that **the single most valuable thing you have is your reputation** and that even the appearance of wrongdoing destroys your reputation. **This is NOT an approach you should take.** It is **never right to violate your integrity.**

Reasoning from first principles; What makes a decision unethical?

First, we need to define things a little. Is it unethical to eat chickens? How about spanking a child? How about causing pollution? Too broad a definition becomes useless.

To be unethical or immoral is to cause unnecessary harm or suffering to others. There are specific legal principles which come into play which should be a part of your process. Going to jail for a "crime" which causes no one any harm still harms you and your reputation.

Sometimes harm to one is necessary to help another. We all must eat to survive. The child needs guidance (though spanking may be the wrong approach). **It is immoral to cause <u>unnecessary</u> suffering.**

Is it ethical to burn coal, profit from the sale and mining of the coal and leave the "external" costs such as carbon emissions, mining tailings, lung diseases, etc. to be borne by other people? **Make sure the options you create pass this fundamental test** first.

Risks

 *"Risk comes from not knowing what you are doing"*

Warren Buffet

Every decision carries positive and negative risks. Be ready to deal with either type.

Start with overall risks that affect every project, decision and life in general. This is the sort of risks we generate for ourselves by being human.

We have behaviors that reliably make us stupid. These include lack of sleep, working under too much stress, trying to do too many things at once, under the influence of alcohol or drugs, snap judgements for choices that have consequences beyond the moment and having biases which impact our judgement. Please refer to the "Eliminate Stupid" page at: https://fapray.com/eliminate-stupid/ for ways to deal with this type of risk.

For the purpose of general risk management consider the standard set by the Project Management Institute in the *"Project Management Body of Knowledge"* 6th edition, used to manage the risks in project decisions.

Manage global risk first

Once you've done what you can do to eliminate stupid, there are still things you can do to manage your overall risk tolerance level to allow you to take properly calculated risks to your own advantage.

Risks

Human beings are not well equipped to cope with risks because of the biases we have evolved over millennia. While the environment has changed for us, our biases lead us to make poorer choices than we would make rationally. They also stress us unnecessarily.

A useful strategy I've found is to have a "Safe Cache" which is a certain amount which is not subject to being risked. **Consider this as a "STOP LOSS Order** for the decision. This assures your minimum amount left in your bank account that you won't risk so you can pay the bills. Once you have established that amount, you can feel confident in the further investments you make. Author Tim Ferris describes his investment strategy as a barbell strategy with one end of the barbell intended to be in safe investments like government bonds that are intended just to keep up with inflation and otherwise minimize risk. The other end of the barbell is invested in high risk – high potential return areas.

The next global thing you can do about risks is to **eliminate or reduce the downside** and increase the upside. There are a lot of ways to help reduce the down side. You can take steps to avoid the risk altogether, mitigate or reduce the risk when it can't be avoided, hedge your bets with insurance or some other strategy, share the risks with others in return for a part of the upside or for a fee, or simply absorb the risk and take the hit if it comes to pass. **Setting trigger points and actions** to take will also give you a viable "plan B".

If you can **take away most of the down side** for your decisions, projects, investments and life you will have invested your time much more wisely than trying to get the "optimum" upside.

Reduce the risks for individual options

Identify various types of negative and positive risks for each individual option and the things which will trigger action to deal with the risks. Determine the likelihood of the risk events. Determine the impact if a risk occurs and decide how to respond to the event if the risk trigger happens. Identifying positive risks helps you to be better prepared to capitalize on opportunities that might also present themselves.

Keep a Risk and Issues log to track the risks you've identified and to capture the trigger points and action plans.

Sample Risk Log

In the example below, we're tracking a risk of price fluctuations, either positive or negative, of materials for our company. If the price fluctuates by 5% in either direction, we've set up a trigger to notify the proper people to follow the action plan. For a price drop of 5%, the action plan calls for us to lock into a long term supply contract. This allows us to take advantage of something that for us was a positive risk.

For the negative version, assume the prices rose by 5%. We'd minimize damage to the company by passing on the price increase to our customers. This has a negative impact on our sales so we need to be careful about how we do it, but sharing even a part of the loss with them (without losing customers) is a win for the company. We have successfully minimized the negative impact.

Risk#	Risk Description	Probability	Impact	Risk Trigger	Action Plan
1	Price fluctuation	High	Medium	5% change	Lock in gains, adjust retail price
2	Supplier labor strike	High	High	Strike vote	Pre stage supplies, insurance, alternate supplier

For the second risk, there are only negative consequences of the risk and it has both a high probability and a high impact. The approach to take here is to assume the risk will occur and avoid it if possible. If avoidance won't be possible, reduce or mitigate the effects of the risk. You can do this with strategies such as reducing your risk exposure by hedging or buying insurance, finding alternate ways to accomplish the tasks needed, limiting the amount of damage the issue will cause. When a risk becomes a reality, it's no longer called a risk, it's now an issue. Sometimes the best or only approach to an issue is to simply suck it up and take the hit. If you're going to be in that position, risk reserves set aside in the planning stage will help cope with the damage and keep you on course.

Some risks are medium or low impact and low probability. Even the lowest probability events happen sometimes so a risk reserve is used to manage their impacts. Risk reserves are money, time or resources set aside during risk planning to manage the effects of negative risk events that could not be anticipated. They allow you to lump the medium and low impact/low probability risks into a single more manageable lump.

Resilience

Give serious consideration to resilience. It should be a component of every project and decision. Is this something that can recover from unexpected events. In business, you need to have a disaster recovery plan and a continuity of business plan. How will you deal with weather events? Do you have a key player succession plan? How are you going to bounce back after the fire/flood/quake/tornado/ice storm?

The IT world deals with resilience on a daily basis. **Every physical part in the universe eventually fails.** Systems are designed so that they have redundancy, automatic failovers, hot standby systems, alternate routing schemes and lots of other methods to distribute loads, fight off hackers and so on.

For your decisions, what is your "plan B"? How will you move forward when "x" goes wrong? Risk management is a part of that planning but risk management can only work for those things which can be anticipated. Resilience includes the ability to fail gracefully, with plenty of warning to let people know of the problems. It includes an assumption that things WILL fail and that you should automatically account for that in your decision making.

Using standardized and off-the-shelf equipment wherever possible also contributes to resilience. If a server goes down and another can be put in place quickly by just loading software, down time is reduced.

Monitoring and awareness is a big part of resilience. Knowing when things are starting to go off course, out of tolerance or when storage is getting full allows for time to respond before the failure occurs. This is also true for organizations and teams. Know when things are starting to go wrong in teams allows you to intervene.

Personal Resilience

Build resilience into your decisions. Build an environment that supports success.

Commitment to each other- When the shit has hit the fan, as has happened quite a few times since Donna and I got married 33 years ago, this made a huge difference. I don't know if either of us would have survived and neither would have thrived without it. Donna has gone through breast cancer a couple of times, I've had major setbacks with work, including 8 months without a job and the very real possibility of losing our home. We've had major surgeries, illnesses and issues with our mental health including depression. Luckily for both of us, we are both truly and deeply invested in the welfare and happiness of the other. Donna is a real momma bear when it comes to protecting her family. I am capable of doing absolutely anything to protect her. Together, we are VERY tough.

Kick Bad Habits - If you start out with bad habits like smoking, as I did, you slowly poison yourself and destroy your own life. I learned that I could take it a step farther and develop habits that were not only "not bad" but that made my life incrementally better over time. First, I had to fix the truly terrible habits. For me, that was quitting smoking. I soon found out that it wasn't going to be easy but when I finally committed to myself to do it, I was able to quit cold turkey. It took everything I had in me over a period of months to get there. I lied to everyone around me including myself for literally years before I finally managed to quit for good.

Avoid easily foreseeable problems. (Risk Management 101) - Once I quit smoking I got very lucky and figured out for myself that I have a somewhat easily addicted personality. That is why I avoid gambling, PC gaming, porn (although I still enjoy nude women I strictly limit porn consumption) and any other thing I can identify that might have addictive properties - including social media. I am susceptible to the small, intermittent rewards that are so seductive about those things so I avoid them.

Personal Resilience

Develop Good Habits - Change your environment to support the changes. Adopt a shelter dog to help you to exercise more. I get at least a mile or so every day in walking our dog, no matter the weather. Another habit I've established is effective exercise every other day. When things were at their worst I upped the exercise in the dojo and gym to keep myself sane. It works. Try to work with your hands at least a little every day. It might be household maintenance or it might be stained glass. Set aside some time every day to learn something or teach something. Try to tackle learning things that are harder rather than easier. If it's easy, anyone can do it. You want to be the guy who sets himself apart by his work ethic.

Build a Support System - Again, your environment drastically affects your habits and can support good one. Get your family and friends on board when you decide to make a change. Have them hold you accountable and cheer you on.

Remember that **hard times are not permanent**. No matter how tough today seems, it will always get better. **Also, don't take hard times personally**. The universe throws things at all of us. We all get old and die. We all lose friends and family. Life was never fair but we can take joy in the good things and realize that losing a job or a spouse, getting sick or injured are not punishments for you in particular, just the way things happen.

Planning and preparation

The boy scout motto is "Be Prepared". You can save yourself and your family a ton of grief and you can save yourself tons of money if you always come prepared. It has always been my unofficial motto in just navigating through life.

I'm not a "prepper" in the sense that I'm not preparing for the end of civilization while sort of hoping I can live in some macho fantasy world where the person with the biggest gun rules the roost. In fact, that's a very nasty place to want to be. Much better to live in a world where your neighbors are your friends and you **work together to make a better world for us all**.

Personal Resilience

We each have a responsibility to self, family and our community to take care of yourself and family during an emergency and to not become a burden. To be able to do that, **put aside emergency tools and supplies** for several weeks. It is too obvious that a major weather event like the tornado that hit Joplin could put us in need of food, water, shelter and tools, medicine, communications and other support which wouldn't be immediately available for some time.

Carry tools in the car in case of a breakdown. When Nick was a baby we had a breakdown in mid-winter while traveling in Iowa. I had blankets, tools and flares so we were never in danger or even very uncomfortable as we waited several hours for help.

When taking on a new job, do the groundwork in advance. Don't reinvent the wheel. Get a new gig and dive in immediately to truly understand all of the ins and outs of the job. Document what you learn as you go. This helps when you have to refer back later to figure out some complex process.

All of this leaves out the most important preparation you can make. Prepare yourself.

Prepare yourself physically so you can be effective and strong enough to help others. You don't need to be superman or supergirl but you do need to be the person who can walk a few miles carrying a load, help carry a stretcher, swim, run, bike a decent distance and generally keep yourself healthy.

Prepare yourself mentally. Push yourself hard and challenge yourself. It is worth it. Stoicism is a great start to prepare yourself mentally. It helps to be mentally tough. When I was in the Marine Corps, I learned the very important lesson that I have the ability to push myself far, far beyond the point where most people would quit. That toughness also means that I can do the hard, dirty work that others don't want to do or that they charge exorbitant amounts to do for you. Learn how to do things for yourself. Simple plumbing, cooking, sewing, electrical work and so on. I ended up being an excellent handyman after a lifetime of fixing things but I also gained a tremendous amount of self-reliance and well earned self respect. Self respect is necessary but meaningless unless it is based on actual achievements.

Bad things will happen. Be prepared for them. Good things will happen, be prepared to take advantage of them. Things you have no control over will affect your life. Be prepared to deal with them.

> Resilience is all about being able to overcome the unexpected. **Sustainability is about survival.** The goal of resilience is to thrive.
> - Jamais Cascio

Perhaps the sustainability chapter should be before the Resilience chapter. **You need to be able to survive before you can thrive.** Oddly, sustainability isn't normally included when you discuss decision making. This isn't because it's unimportant but because people don't associate decision making with sustainability issues. In fact, every decision we make has the potential to lead to a change. Every change has some sort of impact to sustainability.

For example, when considering a project, has there been serious thought given to waste reduction, recycling of materials, reuse of existing materials? Is the energy use of this project as efficient as it could be? Are materials sourced from sustainable sources? Are transport and shipping minimized?

Reduce, reuse and recycle have been the mantra for decades but **sustainability goes beyond these basic personal steps we all can take**. Things like proper disposal of electronics waste from an office upgrade or the recycling of fleet vehicles might **require political leadership as well as good science to discover the most sustainable approach and then to enable it.** Dumping waste into the oceans or shipping it overseas isn't sustainable .

Ethical and Moral Considerations

This also becomes an **ethical consideration** for your company. Remember Caesar's instruction to his wife to avoid even the appearance of impropriety. This is true for every company as well. When viewed by a factual but totally unsympathetic audience, would this decision stand up to scrutiny as the lead article on the Huffington Post?

Even if you have convinced yourself that global warming is not a man-made phenomenon, **does it make any sense to keep throwing gasoline onto the fire that's burning your house down with you trapped inside it**?

There are plenty of sustainability resources such as "[Cradle to Cradle | William McDonough & Michael Braungart](#)". They dive into the ways that we must start to turn around our processes to make our systems sustainable.

In the end, if you don't make sustainability part of your decision making process, you become part of the problem. Be a part of the solution.

Opposing Views

Consider opposing views carefully - Assign a "Devil's Advocate"

Opposition views give you an excellent guardian against confirmation bias. Cherish them and use them to sharpen your logic. Consider the possibility of assigning a person on your team to formally take on the role of "Devil's Advocate. Of course, it might make good sense to let the team know that this is an assigned position meant to strengthen the overall decision. Otherwise your "Devil's Advocate" can end up being socially punished for repeatedly taking unpopular stands. Make certain that everyone knows that once the final decision is reached, no matter what positions were taken during the process, it's now "Our" decision.

What must be true?

Here's a very powerful tool you can use to help correct for confirmation bias and from overconfidence. "What must be true in order for this decision to be the correct one?" Answering this question for each option as you consider it will help to surface issues you might not otherwise perceive. You should also ask the related questions: "What is the probability that all of the necessary conditions will turn out to be true?" and "What is your confidence in those probabilities?" Asking those questions gets you a probability map for each option and approaches it from a perspective that helps keep people from getting too invested in a particular outcome.

Review With Others

You'll also find this thought mentioned in the "Eliminate Stupid" section. A very common mistake to make is to skip the step of peer review. Any serious or complex decision needs to be **reviewed by competent others**. This may mean a formal peer review or it might just mean having someone who was not a part of the original decision making process take a deep dive into the decision.

I stressed "competent others" because this is not a copy editor review looking for grammar errors. It is a review of the decision process with an agenda to surface errors, remaining open questions, misguided assumptions and unrealistic probability estimates. Make certain the people conducting the review are **competent in this domain** or have resources with the right competencies.

This is the point in the process where the ***Decision Log*** you kept as you worked through the options will be most heavily used. Provide the reviewer(s) with the ***Decision Log*** as well as the the decision draft up to this point.

If you are in an environment where you are not the sole decision maker, you should have been keeping the other stakeholders for this decision involved throughout the process. They should be brought up to speed and negotiations started for acceptance of the decision. Bargaining in good faith with the stakeholders will help you to gain acceptance of the ultimate decision and a transparent process with each sub-decision along the way properly documented will help you get buy-in from them. You will need that support to implement the decision so don't give this process less than the full attention it deserves.

Record The Decision

When the review process is complete, you should record the decision in the **Decision Log.**

Keep the decision log on hand so that it can be reviewed once either the success criteria or failure criteria for the decision have been met.

Remember that you also **set risk triggers** early in the process and they should continue to be monitored until the decision has been shown to succeed, fail or be cancelled. If a risk trigger happens, it's no longer considered a risk. It's now called an issue and tracked to resolution in the **Issues Log**, a separate document. Follow the action plan you had created for that risk and communicate the issue to the team.

6

CHAPTER SIX

Learn From Results

The Review

After success or failure trigger, review the decision <u>process</u> to improve it.

The decision or decisions you made should have been captured in a Decision Log or Decision Workbook. After enough time is passed to determine how it has turned out, you should **spend some effort to improve things for the next round.**

The debriefing creates a positive feedback loop or "flywheel"effect which basically means your future decisions will be no worse than the ones you've just made and they will get incrementally better with more experience.

Even the best decisions are rarely perfect given that we start with imperfect information and unpredictable events as the decision is being implemented. If your most recent decision was successful, take a little time to review it and capture any lessons learned from the experience. If those lessons would apply broadly, make sure to incorporate them into your decision making process.

If the decision was unsuccessful, take a deeper dive and determine if the decision itself was wrong. **Sometimes good decision still result in the wrong outcomes.** If the decision was good at the time it was made and if there's no process change that would have improved it, then leave your process alone.

However, if it turns out that the decision was bad, start doing a **root cause analysis.** Ask "why" did it not work and keep asking why until you arrive at the cause of the error. Once you know the root cause, improve your process to capture and correct this type of error.

This turns your entire process into an effective algorithm that improves with experience.

7

CHAPTER EIGHT

Conclusion

Once the review is completed you have come full circle, back to the beginning of the next decision. **Hopefully, you have improved the process** a little so you start out with an even better process for making consequential decisions this time around.

Good decision making skills are essentially the ability to follow a process or algorithm which guides the thought process. If the algorithm itself is good and if you execute it properly, it not only guides your present decisions but will improve with experience to be a better guide in the future.

There is more to a good decision than just following a logical progression. You need the critical thinking skills to comprehend the information you're receiving and to tell the difference between different versions of the same set of facts. You need to be able to detect and filter out baloney, be able to view the problem from different angles and understand the perspectives of different stakeholders. You'll need excellent communication skills to make sure the decision is properly implemented.

While this concise guide should be a great starting point to improve your skills, it is not comprehensive by any means. See the resources section for further reading and great tools.

We hear a lot about the need for "Critical Thinking" skills and most people seem to believe that they have the skills themselves... If only it were true. It's difficult to pass on something you don't understand yourself so the next generation will have to pull themselves up by their own bootstraps. However, there is hope. You have just read through this guide and you should have a good grasp of the process.

Teach Everything You Know!

THANK YOU FOR YOUR TIME. IT'S THE MOST PRECIOUS GIFT OF ALL.

8

CHAPTER SEVEN

Resources

For More Information

1. FAPray.com is my website which contains more on decision making, Advice your Dad would want you to know and project management.
2. "Learning How To Learn" This is a free online course intended to help everyone trying to master complex new skills. Make this short extra effort before starting to learn any new thinking skills and you'll learn much more efficiently. Very Highly Recommended.
https://www.coursera.org/learn/learning-how-to-learn/
3. Learn basic statistics and probability calculation. Without that understanding, we are completely out of our element in the world of random chance, determining how likely something may be or knowing what problems we most need to prepare for. Take an introductory statistics course such as those offered online by the Khan Academy.
https://www.khanacademy.org/math/statistics-probability
4. Read *"The Baloney Detection Toolkit"* This is a tool created for young members of the Skeptic Society to help them distinguish fact from non-fact, whether deliberate or unintentional. It's a good start to reducing the garbage at the inputs. It's a quick and worthwhile read. - Visit the Skeptic Society website at:
https://www.skeptic.com/skepticism-101/baloney-detection-kit-sandwich-infographic/
5. Now that the preliminary groundwork is laid, read *"Rationality: From AI to Zombies"* by Eliezer Yudkowski. Machine Intelligence Research Institute. It is available in an Amazon Kindle Edition. It's also available on the "Less Wrong" Blog. Visit the website and spend quality time there but buy the book on Kindle to support Eliezer's work.
https://www.lesswrong.com/
6. The "Wait But Why" website of Tim Urban is an unparalleled resource for relatable explanations. Tim is a master explainer. When I grow up I want to think like Eliezar Yudkowski and explain things like Tim!
https://waitbutwhy.com/
7. Dr. Gleb Tsipursky and his team of disaster avoidance experts has a wonderful new book out: "**Never Go With Your Gut**"
His website at: https://disasteravoidanceexperts.com/ is a terrific resource.
8. Tim Ferriss is a blogger and author whose work includes "The Tim Ferriss Show", available wherever you get your podcasts. His book "The Tao of Seneca" is an excellent grounding into the stoic philosophy and an enjoyable read. It's available in hardcover, audiobook and as a FREE pdf file to read on your Kindle or laptop. https://tim.blog/2017/07/06/tao-of-seneca/
9. Ryan Holiday has created a mountain of stoic resources. His daily newsletter is a must read. https://dailystoic.com/

Better Decision Checklist

Before you start
- Eliminate the things that make us stupid
- Verify that the decision will support your strategy
- Limit your losses

Define the problem
- What is the problem to be solved?
- Why is the decision needed?
- Clear problem statement
- Stakeholders engaged
- Success and failure criteria defined

Expand options
- Consider the "Do Nothing" option
- Invert the problem
- Brainstorm effectively
- Look for partial solutions and recombine options
- Get expert advice
- Benchmark

Refine the options
- Consider 2nd and 3rd order impacts
- Ethical and moral dimensions
- Evaluate risks and mitigate negative risk
- Plan for sustainability and resilience
- Set risk triggers and action plans
- Set failure and success triggers
- Consider opposing views carefully
- Assign a "Devil's advocate"
- What must be true for a successful outcome
- Review with competent others
- Negotiate and bargain for buy-in

After the decision
- Record the decision results
- After success or failure trigger, review the decision process to improve it.

Risk Log Template

ID	Risk Statement	Risk Description	Assigned To	Planned Completion Date	Closed Date	Severity H, M, L	Likelihood H, M, L	Risk Treatment (a. - j.)	Status

Issue Log Template

ID	Issue Statement	Issue Description	Release	Type	Submitter	Date Submitted	Assigned to	Planned Completion Date

ID	Problem Description	Option	Stakeholders	Success Criteria	Failure Criteria	Assumptions	Decision

> "On an important decision one rarely has 100% of the information needed for a good decision no matter how much one spends or how long one waits. And, if one waits too long, he has a different problem and has to start all over. This is the terrible dilemma of the hesitant decision maker."
>
> — Robert K. Greenleaf, The Servant as Leader

About The Author

Tony Pray is the author of the popular "Things Your Dad Wants You To Know" blog. A former Marine with varied careers ranging from truck driver to blacksmith, lineman to home energy auditor to Sr. IT Project Manager. Mr. Pray teaches Project Management, Critical Thinking Skills and Aikido, plays guitar and lives with his wife and various animals in Kansas.

I am a lifelong seeker of better ways to do everything. I don't want to reinvent the wheel so I find, curate and distill the best of the best current knowledge, best practices, tips, hacks and science to help you navigate.

You can find out more on my blog FAPray.com

Download your FREE

Better Decision Workbook

An excellent tool to begin putting your decisions into action! An Excel spreadsheet template you can use as-is or modify freely.

Send my free workbook!

FAPray.com

Your Turn!

FAPray.com

www.ingramcontent.com/pod-product-compliance
Lightning Source LLC
Chambersburg PA
CBHW061805070526
44586CB00023B/2723